H̲ᴮᵘᵗ...ᴺᵃᵏᵉᵈONEST?

Conversational Foreplay for Dating
Asking the Hard Questions Upfront

H But...Naked ONEST?

Conversational Foreplay for Dating
Asking the Hard Questions Upfront

Troy L. Rawlings

Copyright ©2013 Troy L. Rawlings
Vanglorious Writings Inc.

All rights reserved.

ISBN: 978-0-9769772-9-2

www.butnakedhonest.com
www.troy-ghosthost.com

Publisher's Note:

This publication is designed to provide accurate and authoritative information in regard to the subject matter covered in the author's perspective. It is sold with the understanding that the publisher is not engaged in rendering psychological, financial, legal, or other professional services. If expert assistance or counseling is needed, the services of a competent professional should be sought.

Cover design by Chris Hopkins - www.chrishopkinsdesign.com
Author photo by Debra Simmons - www.diamonddustphotography.com

Edited by: Jessica Tilles - www.twasolutions.com
Interior design by Jessica Tilles - www.twasolutions.com

Printed in the United States of America

Without limiting the rights under copyright reserved above, no part of this publication may be reproduced, stored in or introduced into a retrival system, or transmitted, in any form or by any means (electronic, mechanical, photocopying, recording or otherwise), without the prior written permission of both the copyright owner and the above publisher of this book.

The scanning, uploading, and distribution of this book via the Internet or via any other means without permission of the publisher is illegal and punishable by law. Please purchase on authorized electronic editions and do not participate in or encourage piracy of copyright materials. Your support of the author's rights is appreciated.

DEDICATION

*I dedicate this book to the memory of
my beginning and to the promise of my future.*

*This is dedicated to my father,
Harold Delroy Rawlings Sr. Rejoice in Heaven Dad!*

*And to my beautiful daughter, Zoe Troi Rawlings.
Continue to prosper in Love and Life JuJu!*

TABLE OF CONTENTS

Foreword 9

Introduction 11

1 Your Past 17

2 Individuality 23

3 The Meeting 27

4 The Next Day Phone Call 39

5 1st Date 47

6 Deep Water or the Shallow End 57

7 The Big Joker aka The Crazy Card 65

8 The Beef 79

9 The Decision 89

10 Bonus Blogs: Sex & Love Raw Uncut 95

FOREWARD

This heartfelt piece of work has all the ingredients for a great relationship.

Troy has gone up against the grain, letting women and men know, up front, what is expected of them emotionally.

This is what you need to do to make a relationship not only work but thrive on every level.

I was blown away just from the title. This is a "must have" for any relationship that wants to be outstanding.

—Yonder, Author of the *What I Do Is Taboo* series
www.whatidoistaboo.com

Introduction

WHAT IS MY REASON FOR WRITING this book, you ask? Well, the answer is simple. I have something to say to the world about relationships that may help some people. Keyword—SOME! I know there are some who aren't ready to try radical ideas when it comes to dating and long-term relationships. But, those who are will experience a newfound bliss and freedom that will change their lives forever.

Have you ever noticed that a naked baby never tries to hide his nakedness? I mean, he just lays there rolling

"But...Naked Honest?"

around happy, free, nothing but naked! In fact, if the parent doesn't put a diaper on him, he will do his "do" all over the place and continue to roll in fun. For obvious safety and societal reasons, we are taught to hide our nakedness as we grow from infant to toddler to adolescent to adult. We are also taught by circumstances and heartbreaks to cover our emotions. While this is a necessary safety measure at times, as well, I believe we sometimes hide our feelings to the point of losing part of our humanity. Our emotions are a big part of what makes us human.

In this modern day and time, people have stopped using certain words and phrases that seem too emotional. For example, instead of saying "I apologize," people will say "My bad!" Or, instead of saying "My feelings were hurt…you hurt my feelings…" they will say "I felt some kind of way about that…" Funny at times, but sad also, is that we seem not to want to show the world the depths of whom we are. We are terrified of being embarrassed or humiliated by some of the most basic aspects of our

Introduction

life. So, if we are this fearful of everyday interaction and communication with each other, shouldn't it be obvious why so many relationships are failing, and better yet... non-existent?

The most important component to a good relationship is communication. I believe the more open and honest the communication between you and your partner, the better your relationship will be. Now, I didn't say this would be easy or that starting to be totally honest with your mate will turn your relationship around overnight. Actually, if you say the wrong thing it could end your relationship. So, be careful.

I enjoyed my stand-up comedy years. What I loved the most about doing stand-up comedy—well second to making people laugh—was that the stage made me honest. It was the perfect truth serum. I started to realize the more transparent I was with the audience the more they connected to what I was saying and to me. The more honest I was the more genuine my performance. I began to use the same approach in everyday life, being more transparent to build better relationships. Telling the truth about my past, who I am and especially what I wanted proved to be a strong key to success. In dating relationships, this proved to reduce drama and heartache greatly.

Now, let me be clear with you. I wasn't a blatant liar who was a menace to the dating society. Personally, I wanted to be a better person. And, I wanted to give the person I was interested in dating all the necessary information to decide if she wanted to deal with me. If not, she could choose "No" and still be cool, calm and cordial; not finding out something down the road that caused her to leave our relationship.

In the chapters of this book are techniques on how to talk about some of the hardest topics with your partner or would-be mate. Those things—if they were to come up later in a marriage or a relationship could possibly cause you to get a divorce or breakup. Things like your

Introduction

past, sexual preferences and what you're looking for in a long-term relationship. I will also break down how to get to know some important facts about a person early in the dating process. Even though only time reveals certain things about a person, you should have a firm foundational knowledge about the person you're dating and vice versa. When you have this knowledge, you can decide if this is a person you want to have a long-term relationship with, friendship or just a cup of coffee.

Chapter 1

Your Past

ALL OF US HAVE A PAST. SOME more scandalous than others, but all of us have good, bad and ugly things that mold us into the people we are. It's not how crazy your past is, as much as if you are comfortable with your past that matters most. Have you come to terms with what you went through? Have you made peace in your heart about how you were treated? A wise person once said, "Hurt people hurt people." That is true. If you have been hurt and become bitter and don't get help, counseling, or deal with it in some way, you could transfer that hurt to someone else.

DADDY & MOMMY

Our first influences—the first people we learn from—are, of course, our parents. What did you see in your parents' relationship growing up? Were there arguments, fights, and violence or was it a peaceful, loving household? Were you raised in a single-parent household? You may be asking, "Troy, what does that have to do with anything?" Well, it has a lot to do with everything you go through in your relationships with a would-be mate, or even a friend. For example, the young lady who grew up without a father figure, and was raised by her mother or another woman could have a negative image of men if there was never a strong, male role model in her life. It may be hard for her to adjust to a man who is strong in his ways because he may seem harsh and brash. Or, if a man is a gentleman who likes to open doors and cater to his lady, there could be friction there, as well. She may want to continue to open her own doors. If a young man grew up with just his father or saw his mother abused, he could have a very disrespectful attitude toward women. If he did not learn how to be respectful to the first woman in his life, his mother, he may have a very hard time respecting a girlfriend.

ABUSE

Those who were emotionally or sexually abused may carry a certain type of caution into a new relationship. Those who have been abused could have at least three types of pain to overcome: the pain of the actual abuse, the pain of the embarrassment that people may know or find out about it, and the painful fear of it happening again. Abuse can leave a scar so deep that sometimes the true effects don't reveal themselves until later in a relationship. From my experience, I've learned the emotional abuse I endured as a teenager from my parents' bad habits and the dissention in their relationship, affected how I deal with my relationships to this day. Thoughts flow through my mind like *Can I Trust this person? Will they judge me when I tell them my likes and dislikes? Will they be there when I need them to hold my heart for me?* "Hold my heart" meaning what I tell them in the most private times won't come back and slap me in the face in an argument. They won't use my weaknesses against me, rather they'll lift me up when I'm down, and encourage me when my courage is lacking.

If you've suffered any type of abuse, some type of therapy is necessary. Take time to find a good therapist, psychiatrist, counselor, or somebody who has been trained in dealing with your specific type of abuse. What do you have to lose? It is important for us to have someone to open up to about what we've gone through, especially if you see a pattern of damaging habits that might have been the result of the abuse. Talking about it can bring healing from it. But it's up to you how soon, in the stages of a relationship, you choose to reveal these portions of your past. There is no definitive timeline. You have to feel comfortable enough with the past and the person to say, "Okay, here's something that happened to me that I want you to know." Sometimes, the thing that seems to be the biggest obstacle from your past, once it's revealed, can lead to the biggest breakthrough in your future.

CHEATING

A hard past issue to overcome is cheating. When you find out your mate has cheated, you become the Cheating Expert. An infidelity Inspector! You begin to retrace every step or characteristic you noticed the cheater displayed. Sad to say, this is not fair to the person you're interested in dating now, nor yourself. But, who could blame you? When your trust has been destroyed by someone you truly love, it can leave you devastated! And, when you get the strength and courage to move forward and try to date again, you obviously want to avoid the same result. So, you make a

"But...Naked Honest?"

vow that is extremely hard to keep, if not impossible. You say to yourself, "I will never experience that pain again!" but that could be a false promise to yourself. I believe it is impossible to love fully with your guard up. Nothing in the world makes you more vulnerable than LOVE. You're bound to experience some pain, and/or discomfort because your heart and feelings are exposed. And, once again, in the pursuit of relationship happiness, you have to learn to trust and be open.

All of these factors play a role in how you view dating and relationships. Your past has brought you to your present. How you grow and learn from it, or not, will shape your future.

Chapter 2

Individuality

THE MOST POWERFUL TRAIT I'VE LEARNED and embraced over the years is the importance of individuality. Not just my own, but everyone else's, as well. It helps me cut down on judging others so harshly because they don't think like me. How arrogant of me to get mad, frustrated, and dismissive to some folks because they don't think like me? If we all thought alike, acted alike and looked alike, we'd lose it. And, the world would be a very boring place. With that said, I'm not suggesting you throw your 'personal preference list' (for your future mate) away, especially when it comes to morals and bad habits. If you aren't interested in someone who smokes, you don't have to overlook a habit that could be dangerous to your health and your partner's. Your partner's individuality should attract you to them, not repel you away.

RESPOND/REACT

By accepting someone's individuality, you can be less critical of their decisions. As you get to know someone, they reveal to you how they react in certain situations. When their back's against the wall, when they're mad, sad, depressed, happy, horny, nervous, fearful…whatever the case, you will learn, over time, the depths of this person. If you already have in mind that they are going to be who they are, then you will allow them to show you who they really are. And, when they're comfortable that you are not going to judge them or put undue expectations on them,

Individuality

they will kick their "Representative" to the curb, and REVEAL THE REAL! Like I'd mentioned earlier in the book, and will do throughout, it does take time to know the depths of a person. It could take a lifetime. My goal in *But Naked…* (aka Butt Naked) is to help you get and give as much important information up front, as possible. And I believe it's very important to identify how we respond and react to everyday comments and situations, as well as the hard times in life. If we pay attention, it shows us our important personality traits. Why did you fly off the handle when that person made that joke? Or, why do you feel that way about that restaurant or that part of town? Or, why is that particular thing or topic taboo to you? All of these things have a core. A place of origin in our minds and hearts where the reason we react the way we do stems from. Although at times it may be hard to talk about, it's necessary to know so it doesn't cause constant turmoil in our relationships.

JUST BEING ME

A girl I once dated told me, "I don't like your facial expressions," and she was dead serious! So that was the end of that rendezvous. Certain things we say and do will never change. Those little quirks make us the individuals we are. Facial expressions, how we laugh, how we smile, our voice, the way we walk—even things we tend to like to say and do without thought—are all character traits that usually don't change much without surgery or enhancement. If you don't like something about someone that is a permanent characteristic of theirs, don't lie to yourself, time is probably not going to change it.

Ask yourself, "Do I like this person just the way they are?" If the answer is yes then you're free to continue on the journey, but if the answer is no, run away…or proceed with caution.

Chapter 3

The Meeting

SO NOW, WE GET INTO THE meat of it all. Or, should I say, the "meet" of it all. Every day we have an opportunity to meet new and interesting people who may or may not become a part of our lives in some way. From the time you leave your house in the morning, your life starts connecting, if you allow it to, with hundreds of people. Jogging, traffic, your coffee/breakfast spot, newspaper stand, children's school, work, lunch break, supermarket, gas station, night club, or church…all you have to do is spark up or engage in conversation with someone and the possibilities are endless. Now, try not to read this book, then go out, and be *Ms. or Mr. So-Damn-Excited-to-Talk-to-Everybody!* Take it easy, relax, and, most of all, be yourself when meeting someone new. Get used to being yourself from the start. Please, please, please leave your "Representative" at home from now on. Let people see you enjoying everyday life, or even a little upset if the day is not going too well. Ladies and gentlemen, be open to someone cheering you up, giving you a compliment, or even offering to buy you a cup of coffee or something. Be a little more generous, as well. You may be the one offering to buy them a house…I mean, dinner. Like I said, relax.

FIRST INTENT

There is a verse in the Bible that says, *Man looks on the outward appearance, God looks on the heart.* Now, in no way do I think that's a bad thing. I believe as human beings, with eyes, the first thing we see is how a person looks.

The Meeting

Some people are attractive to you and some aren't. That's just natural. It's good to know what it is about a person's outward appearance that attracts you to them. His muscular build or her curvaceous figure, her hair, his eyes; what did you notice about them first that drew you to them? Guys, was it her beauty or her booty? Be honest with yourself, it's cool. Her beauty can actually be much more than just her hair and her eyes. What did her smile do to you? Was it her voice that drew you closer? *Merriam-Webster* defines beauty as "Any of those attributes of form, sound, color, execution, character, behavior, etc., which give pleasure and gratification to the senses or to the mind."

As many of you probably know and have heard; men are very visual creatures. What we see tends to excite us or turn us off right away. At the same time, we're very sensual. In that first meeting, a man's senses go crazy when he sees and meets a woman he's attracted to. Outside of a woman's physical beauty, there is her confidence, sexiness/sex appeal, joy…yes, all these things exude from you like perfume whether you know it or not. There is even a

"But...Naked Honest?"

pheromonal attraction that occurs, without you knowing, that may have you saying, "I don't know what it is about you…"

Now, there is also what I like to call "Booty Attraction." This is when a guy is hunting for a partner based on sexual attraction alone. I'm not going to bash the booty attraction dude at all. Like the tone and title of this book suggests, just be honest with yourself and the woman. That way you save yourselves a lot of drama and heartache moving forward…hopefully. There are times when a guy or a girl is totally honest with what they want at the beginning: "I just want to have fun, someone to kick it with… (a casual sex-friend with benefits)" and the other person has the weird notion that they can change their mind. Let me give a little advice here. Don't try to change someone's mind about what they want. That type of manipulation usually backfires on you. Believe what that person says they want. If you are on the same page, stay. If not, say "No thanks" and walk away.

The Meeting

Ladies, was it his character or his car that attracted you? I hear some women now saying, "Why does it have to be about his car? I'm not that type..." Wait, calm down. Okay, let's say anything that is outwardly attractive about him. His curly hair, his beautiful brown eyes, broad shoulders, tall, dark and handsomeness...whatever made you swoon without reservation. I believe women have an ability to feel deeper, even at the meeting point. Women are usually pegged as "Emotional Creatures." There's nothing wrong with that. But, what I don't like about that is sometimes it makes people think or want to believe women don't get hot and swept away by how a man looks, what he wears or even what he drives. Let's face it; some men wear their cars like a beautiful diamond necklace to adorn their appearance.

Or, was it his character that attracted you? His smile, did he open the door for you or someone else? Did you notice how he talked to a waitress or a friend of his? Did he greet you properly and not come off like a jerk? Not saying that a guy has to approach you first, but I believe there should be a mutual attraction and respect from the beginning. I tell people in my forums and shows all the time, "It better start blissful! There will be enough hardships and obstacles attacking your relationship later on, so start giddy and happy." I believe that to my core. I believe meeting someone should be a fun, interesting, sexy, engaging experience. And if we're honest about our first intent, and can find a way to communicate and even verbalize it, it could be the beginning of a beautiful relationship.

GRAND VERBALIZER

There are times when saying exactly what's on your mind, at the exact time you think it, is not the option and may get you in trouble. Comedians have the ability to take the hard issues and embarrassing situations of life and make them palatable. We make them easy to digest, even amusing because there is truth in jest. The "Grand Verbalizer" is a person who knows how to

The Meeting

communicate the difficult conversations without being shook and rattled about them. This doesn't mean the person doesn't care. It may simply mean they're taking time to process every aspect of the situation and choosing to react in a lighter way than zapping out and throwing a tantrum. Here are a few ways to introduce some "deeper" conversation starters into your first meeting.

1. *"You're here, but where is your significant other?"*— Now, of course, it seems easy enough to ask someone if they are married or if they have a boyfriend or girlfriend. But, sometimes, people have a hard time asking that simple question. I was watching a popular talk show the other day and a young lady in the audience said she was dating a guy four years before she found out he was married. Four years?! Are you telling me that in four years she couldn't figure out he was married? Could she call him twenty-four-seven or were certain times off limits? Did she ever spend a weekend at his house? Better yet, a weeknight? Were they just having

movie dates and sex or was this a serious relationship? Come on now…there had to be a clue somewhere… right? Maybe not. Some folks are just masters of the lie. They are non-Oscar-winning actors out there that just want what they want, and don't mind lying to get it. It's not only sad; it's dangerous for those innocent hearts that are so easily caught up in LOVE. This is something you need to ask as soon as you realize you want this person to be single. If you don't care whether they're single or not, disregard this line of questioning.

2. *"For fun, even though I don't have kids, I like to go to amusement parks." Or, "I love to take my daughter to…"*—Shockingly, some people don't divulge that they have kids upon the first meeting. I figure this should be an initial conversation question: DO YOU HAVE ANY CHILDREN? Now, I understand not letting your children meet new people until you're ready. I totally understand being very selective and cautious when it comes to introducing your child

The Meeting

to a person before you're sure of how long they'll be around. Do you get the sense that I'm serious about not introducing your kids to anyone? Okay, I'll move on. Some of you may think this is a bit much for initial conversation, but I think not. I believe this is light and informative. We tend to drift from topic to topic when first meeting someone anyway. So, in the midst of the randomness, why not find out some very important information? Plus, you may want to pay attention to how this person talks about their children or how they mention not having children.

3. *"Do you have to work tomorrow?"*—Just another polite way of asking, "DO YOU HAVE A JOB?" How does this individual make money? Can they afford the cup of coffee you're about to order? Let me say this clearly. Though money is not everything, it can buy almost everything. It's been widely discussed and many statistics show that the leading causes for divorce and relationship break-ups are sex problems, and

money problems. And, at times, sex is easier to talk about than money. I've found this to be true. Go on a street corner with a camera and ask people personal questions about sex and sexuality and most will giggle, laugh and even go into detail about their wildest adventures. Yet, if you start asking people about their bank account balances or their debt, they'll give you the evil eye. A general conversation starter is asking a person where they work.

I know some of you may be thinking, *That's a lot of information to get when you're just meeting someone. Isn't it?* And, to that, I say, "...to each his own..." You have the power to decide what things you want to know about a person right at the first conversation with them. If you decide just to have fun, mindless chatter, then, by all means, enjoy the bliss of the moment. But, if you'd like to go deeper, these are just a few ways to introduce different lines of questioning…I mean, topics for conversation.

The Meeting

ONE NIGHT STAND

As you look back to see if you've missed something in the paragraphs before this one, let me help you...YES, I SAID ONE NIGHT STAND. Even though this may be unbelievable to some of you, I want to deal with this briefly very early in this short book. It happens. People have met someone and, within that same twenty-four-hour period, had sex with them. Is this smart? I don't think it's the best decision. But, I've met couples who waited to have sex until marriage and are now divorced after one year, and I've met couples who had sex immediately and have now been together more than twenty years. This could deem you promiscuous or a romantic genius, but I feel you have to guard your heart and your body with caution, even in your spontaneity. I felt it necessary to mention this because so many authors don't. And I wanted to talk about it in this "Meeting" chapter because I believe that is when men and women decide or realize that they are or are not sexually attracted to someone.

"But...Naked Honest?"

And chemistry, flirtatious talk and play, and an alcoholic beverage of choice could be all it takes to have you acting on feelings, emotions and hormones. Sex is the most powerful act in the world, outside of love. Sex can draw two people closer, drive them apart, and create life. So while living in the moments of life, just be careful to with whom you choose to share your body, mind and soul. As I mentioned earlier in this chapter, there are endless possibilities when meeting new people, so have fun and don't limit yourself. While, in this book, I'm trying to show you some fun, easy, and, sometimes, surprising ways to talk about the deeper things up front, remember that it's totally up to you to decide how much information you give or ask for when first meeting someone. And, I believe there's no right or wrong way to go about it, if it produces the results you want. However, don't get so consumed with the techniques that you forget to enjoy yourself. Enjoy yourself!

Chapter 4

The Next Day Phone Call

WITH EMAILS, TEXTS, SKYPE, OOVOO, AND holograms, there is no reason not to keep in instant touch with someone you meet. We've over done it a bit. I'm old enough to remember when there were no pagers and the average person remembered at least fifty phone numbers in their head. Even when pagers came about, you had to wait ten to twenty minutes for someone to find a pay phone, if they were available to talk. Now, you meet someone, type their phone number in your phone and call them right in front of them just to make sure they lock you in…and that they didn't give you a fake number…I'm just saying. So, in saying all that, I still believe that if you're truly interested in someone you meet, try to go back to the "Old School" approach of calling them on the phone. It's more intimate when you hear a person's voice and the emotions that every word carries with them.

ALEX'S Q&A

When I was in high school, sometimes I'd stay over with Alex, my cousin. He, his sister, Shelly, and I went to the same high school in Baltimore County, Maryland. I loved spending time at their house; it was like my second home. Alex and I would sleep in the same room and at night, when he talked to his female friends on the phone, he'd talk to them for hours. Actual conversations! He wasn't just listening and grunting a yes or no every now and then, he was in deep dialogue. One night, I asked him, "How do you talk that long on the phone?" And

The Next Day Phone Call

what he told me made perfect sense! He showed me a list of questions that he would ask, and then he would answer them, too. Genius! Alex didn't ask these questions in a mechanical form, and he didn't let the girls know. He used the list to find out key information and as a conversation starter or regenerator if the phone call was dying down. Now, I can't remember Alex's questions, but here are some that you can use:

1. What's your full name?
2. Where are you from?
3. What's your birthday?
4. Where did you go to school?
5. Do you have any pets?
6. What are the longest and shortest relationships you've ever had?
7. What was your most embarrassing moment?
8. What's your favorite movie?
9. What's your favorite dish or food to eat?
10. Where do you see yourself in five years?

"But...Naked Honest?"

These are just ten questions off the top of my head. As you ask your questions, let each one flow into a conversation. (There's a section for Notes in the back of the book) "What's your full name? Oh, that's beautiful…how did your parents come up with that? My mother got my middle name from a soap opera…" You'll soon see that the minutes will just melt away, and you'll be having fun while learning about a new person.

DO YOU LIKE ME? CHECK YES OR NO

Think back to elementary school. Do you remember the little notes that kids would send to possible boyfriends and girlfriends? The notes would say "DO YOU LIKE ME?" and under that question would be three answers with a small box next to each one. The answers were YES, NO, and MAYBE. It's amazing how straight to the point children are, yet it seems sometimes as we get older we get evasive, start lying and dance around certain questions to avoid hurting or getting hurt. One very important thing that the next day phone call does is tell the person that you like them. No need to beat around the bush with this one. Your newfound friend needs to, and wants to, know where they stand with you. This is another chance to be honest and find out how they feel about you, as well.

WE HAVE SO MUCH IN COMMON

While taking mental notes during your first phone conversation, above everything else, you should pick out the things you both have in common. These things will cause you and your new friend to meet on common ground. This will break down some of the invisible walls and allow you both to "let down your hair." Then it will be even easier to discover who your new friend really is. If you find that you have very little in common, you'll have to decide if you want to back off or if you want to learn some new and exciting things. And I can't state this enough: HAVE FUN! This is not an inquisition. You're not interrogating this person; you're trying to get to know the person.

FIRE YOUR REPRESENTATIVE

The first phone conversation is also an excellent time to "Fire Your Representative." Meaning, BE YOURSELF not who you think the other person is looking for. If you're transparent, then it makes it easier for the other person to relax and be more open. You have to be willing to let down your guard a little to discover, and invite in a new friend. And don't be scared to tell them to "Fire your representative when you're talking to me." Many times, I believe we are so caught up in trying to please or appease someone that we miss a great opportunity to connect in a greater way.

MOVE FORWARD OR STEP BACK

In every stage of getting to know someone, there are opportunities to step back or move forward. In this conversation, before you hang up that phone, you should make a definite decision that YES I want to go out on a

The Next Day Phone Call

date with this person or, ummmm, NO…I'll pass. Either way, you're making a sound decision that you should feel good about. Treat getting to know someone like the old school "Choose your Own Adventure" books, the only catch is that you can't go back, flip through some pages and change your decision. Know that when you choose your course, you have to walk it through, good or bad. Get excited and have fun in the good choices, and learn from (don't beat yourself up about) the not so good decisions.

Chapter 5

1ˢᵗ *Date*

I KNOW IT SEEMS LIKE WE took forever to get to the first date, but this is probably just the second day, so calm down. Hopefully, you've received some good info thus far. But, I believe there is nothing more informative, intriguing, or revealing to the senses than being face-to-face with someone you're interested in. This is where you get to express physically how you feel about someone…in the subtlest way…through body language and reaction…

"But...Naked Honest?"

and vice versa. I'm not going to assume that all of you who read this book feel comfortable going on a date, or that you have a failsafe plan in how to conduct yourself each and every time you date. I believe each date is a different experience and should be fun, exciting, romantic and informative. Instead of talking about what I think are the "Do's and Don'ts of Dating" in this chapter, I'm going to give you my "5 Butt-Naked Honest Principles." Hopefully, these will help you, not just on your date, but in life as a whole.

HAPPINESS IS THE SWEETNESS OF LIFE

1. *Happiness is the sweetness of life. Pursuing happiness keeps us alive. Attaining happiness keeps us living!* I truly believe that without happiness we'll just have a meager, short-lived existence, and shrivel up and die depressed and angry. Harsh, huh? Not at all. If you're not happy, what's the purpose of doing... ANYTHING WE DO? If you believe in God then

you know He desires for you to be happy. If you don't know, NOW you know. So, why do some of us settle to be with someone who is either unhappy or who doesn't make us happy? Let me say this, YOU deserve to be happy! No matter your past hurts or mistakes, choose to start being happy today and I guarantee that you will feel better inside and out. You'll even look better. Really! Put happiness into practice immediately. Learn or recover those things that make you happy, those things that aren't damaging to your health, or may kill you, of course. You have to know what makes you happy and put those things in your life. If you're not happy, you can't make anyone happy.

THEY'RE NOT YOU

2. ***If they're not you, don't be mad when they don't think like you!*** Respecting a person's individuality is a key part of building a good relationship. If you find yourself not liking who a person reveals they truly are,

"But...Naked Honest?"

then you don't need this person in your life. There is no reason to try and change someone. If we tried to change to fit everyone's needs, wants, and likes, we'd all be in a mental hospital somewhere. There would be no more schools, prisons, or malls. They would all be replaced with mental hospitals. Seriously, learning how to be comfortable with someone being who they are is very important to not just dating, but any relationship in life. Of course, you're not going to like everything about someone all the time. Ask married couples. Even those who are very happily married will tell you that sometimes their spouse ticks them off. That's just a part of us all being different. If you don't like and love someone for who they are, you just can't like or love them at all.

TREAT HER LIKE A LADY

3. *If she's a female, treat her like a lady.* The legendary R&B soul-singing group The Temptations had a hit

song called "Treat Her Like A Lady." One part of the song goes, "Light the cigarette that she smokes, even help her with her coat." Well she might not smoke cigarettes, but the least you can do is help her put on her coat. Open the car door and any door for her. Some ladies are so used to opening their own doors that they'll slap a man's hand before he can grab the handle, or turn a knob. Pull her chair out so she can sit down at the dinner table. Compliment what she does and how she looks. Chivalry didn't die with knighthood. It's still honorable to be a gentleman, even when it's not expected or accepted. Now, if you don't know what being a gentleman is, start with the things I mentioned in this section. Then go get some books or go online and do a little homework. Treating a woman like a lady will usually bring out the lady in her almost every time.

REALIZE BEFORE RIDICULE

4. ***Give a man a chance to realize the next step before you ridicule him.*** A man's ego is synonymous with a woman's feelings and emotions. Maybe by me saying that more women will realize how the way they speak to a man directly affects what he will do for you and how he will treat you. It may seem to some that nagging, insults and ridicule gets the results they want, but you're damaging your relationship. I believe ridicule is like a slow moving cancer that will eventually kill a relationship. For example, if you would like him to open the car door for you, just wait before you grab the handle. Now, if he is totally clueless and looks at you crazy, simply ask, in your most beautiful lady-like voice, "Can you open the door for me, please?" If he still doesn't get it, say, "I love it when a gentleman opens a door for me." Now if he is interested, in the slightest, in pleasing you, then he will promptly apologize and open the door. After he does it, look him in his eyes and give him a smile and a heartfelt, "Thank you." You

can even throw a "baby" or "sweetie" in there. You're not patronizing him in doing this; you're bringing the gentleman out of him by speaking deeply to his ego. Women, just in case you don't know this let me tell you, not only do you captivate our attention and our sensuality as men because you own the "Sexual Universe," you control the most powerful navigational tool in the world. YOUR TONGUE, if used the right way (what you say and how you say it), will get you anything you want from a man. Sweeten your speech and you'll get more treats.

NEVER FEEL BAD ABOUT BEING YOU

5. *Never feel bad about being yourself!* I can't stress enough being comfortable in your own skin. You have to feel good about being who you are. All your crazy facial expressions, your quirks, bad habits and good. It's better to bring them right to the table, at the beginning, so the person you're dating can know

"But...Naked Honest?"

what they're dealing with right away. Say, "This is who I am. Love me or leave me alone!" One of my mentors said a quote, years ago, that still holds true: "You can change without growing, but you can't grow without changing." Hopefully you're growing into a better you every day. I hope that every day you live striving to be better, to impact the world and the people around you in a positive way all the time. But, even on those days when you don't feel like being happy-go-lucky, never feel bad about being you. The person for you, your future mate, will have to love the good, bad and ugly of you. I always say, "Can they be with you the way you are now or at your worst?" If so, then you want that person in your life.

Whether at the coffee shop, the restaurant, or on that walk in the park, I hope you can reflect on these principles I've given you, as they will make a positive impact on you and your dating experience. There are no quick tricks you can do to get a mate. That takes time. But, if you stay positive about the fun and wonderful part of life that dating and meeting new people can bring, you'll be amazed at how time flies when you're enjoying the moment and having fun. Remember, dating never has to end. Even after marriage, spouses should still enjoy dating each other and discovering new intimacies about each other. Enjoy your dating experience.

Chapter 6

Deep Water or the Shallow End

NOW YOU'VE HAD YOUR FIRST DATE. Let's fast forward a little bit. Let's say you really like this person and you've chosen to keep seeing them for a month or so. Maybe you're trying to make a decision on how deep this relationship is now, and how deep you both want to go. This is natural. You should want to know where you both stand. As feelings and commitment increases, so do expectations. This can be a downer conversation when approached too early and too seriously, like most of what we've covered so far. Here's the tip, don't be scared to take your time! Though you may be dying to know the answers to the following questions, remember if you're not ready for the answers, don't ask.

HOW DO YOU FEEL ABOUT US?

So your new guy or gal is taking up most of your time and all your thoughts. It's no problem to you because you give both freely. Your heart and nose are wide opened, and you think you know how your loved one feels, but do you really? The best way to find out what you want to know is to ask. Hopefully, you both are feeling the same way at the same time. I believe this isn't always the case. I believe the majority of the time, in a relationship, you and your mate won't feel the same way at the same. This interesting dynamic seems to cause so much stress in relationships. Or, maybe it's the almighty "Communication Gap" between men and women. Who knows? The fact is, you will be just fine, as long as you have mutual like or love for each

Deep Water or the Shallow End

other. Think about it. After the bliss and the honeymoon stage have worn off a bit, there will be times when that wonderful creature may rub you the wrong way, or may even piss you off. But, how you feel about each other, at your core, will give you staying power.

What if they don't feel the same way? If this person doesn't feel the same way you do, try not to panic. Over the years, I've had hundreds of conversations with couples from all walks of life, and what always stood out most was who had deeper feelings first. It never fails. Maybe one of you is unsure, maybe its cold feet about moving forward or maybe it's the total fear of the unknown. Relationships are filled with various "unknowns." Unknown obstacles, circumstances, temptations, and trials. Even unknown joyful moments. Yes, some people fear possible happiness. This may seem weird, but if most of your relationships have had sad endings, joy would be a new phenomenon for you. Amazingly enough, you may have made a joyful/happy relationship your chief adversary! You may be sabotaging your own happiness because of fear. So, I'll say that even though you need to know, and you should want to know where you and your mate stand as far as your feelings for each other, it's not an end all if you don't feel the same way at the same time. Take the attitude that your relationship is going to be fine. Don't be scared to let the feelings grow.

HOW DO I MAKE THEM LIKE ME MORE

Even as I typed the title of this section, I said, "REALLY?" But, if I were to be honest, when I was in elementary school, I remember wishing the little girl I had a major crush on FELT THE SAME WAY, TOO! If you ever had a crush on someone, that was your wish. The problem is trying to change a person's mind about how they naturally feel about you is manipulation. Its one thing to let a person's feelings grow naturally as time or admiration progresses, but it's a whole different topic to manipulate one's emotions and feelings. To manipulate

Deep Water or the Shallow End

means to influence someone deceptively. You actually deceive a person into believing something they are not ready to, or don't want to believe or feel. There's no way to lighten this technique or make it sound nicer. That's actually what the whole "Representative" tactic can turn into.

Earlier in the book, I mentioned not bringing your representative to the table. I know for some people, especially some women, your representative may just be a quieter, calmer version of who you really are. And that's not too bad. But, for some people, their representative is a doctor who lives in a plush condo and drives an S-Class Mercedes (which is in the shop) or a Hollywood producer. Or, that young lady who laughs at every one of his jokes and caters to every need until they are in a committed relationship. That's manipulation to get what you think you want, and it usually backfires on both people. One of the main problems with manipulation is if you begin with a lie, or overall deceit, about who you really are, you have

"But...Naked Honest?"

to continue that lie for as long as you're with the person. Let's say the manipulation isn't that big of a lie. You said you like roller coasters, but the very thought of being on a rollercoaster makes you sick to your stomach. When your mate takes you on that blindfolded trip to the biggest amusement park in the world for a date, because he knew you loved to ride roller coasters as much as him, what do you do then? Fake being sick and mess up his surprise?

It's easier to be you and let the person like you just the way you are. If they don't give you all the attention, like, or love you want, then at least you know you did the best at being you that you could do. This also goes for being overly flirty, sensual and sexual with someone when that's not really who you are. Be careful of being a "tease" up front and then turning into a nun or priest later. I know this seems funny, but sometimes desperation makes you suggest or do things you really don't want to.

Take your time, relax, and introduce yourself to the person just the way you are. Who knows, they may fall for you on the spot. What have you got to lose?

I'M DOING 55 THEY'RE DOING 80

Now here is the other side of the coin. You meet someone you enjoy spending time with, but they are moving 80 miles per hour and you're doing 55. This means, they're trying to get to the next stage faster than you are. I have personally learned, as well as from the accounts of others, that if you're not open about how you truly feel when your mate let's you know they're ready to take the relationship to the next level; you can hurt them and yourself in the long run. "But I really like him, I don't want to lose him…" Listen, if he leaves you because you're being honest then he didn't want you; he wanted the thought of wherever he was trying to go. And you don't own anyone but yourself! This is another form of manipulation. Going along with something because of what? Not wanting a person to find what they really want in a relationship? Come on, people. Be fair to you and them. Change is inevitable. Being honest about who you are and where you are with your feelings can actually make the CHANGE of feelings as they grow a wonderful thing. It's like driving. Remember, accidents happen when people merge into traffic too quickly. But, if you pay attention, take your time, and merge into the flow, you both will get to your destination safe and sound.

Chapter 7

The Big Joker aka The Crazy Card

HAVE YOU EVER PLAYED THE CARD game Spades? In some circles, this card game is as religious as brushing your teeth. Four people, who partner in twos, play the game of Spades. Now, the "Big Joker" is the highest card in the deck. No matter what card is played against the "Big Joker," it will win. It takes out the other cards with no problem. But, here's the dangerous thing about the Big Joker. The other players don't know who has it and it usually comes out during the most crucial part of the game. Even a player's partner doesn't know if his partner has the Big Joker.

In a relationship, I like to call a person's craziness the Big Joker or the Crazy Card. I believe we all have some craziness about us. Sometimes, it may be a weird laugh, a facial expression, or tick. Or, the way someone handles fear, being angry or any other emotion. The problem we face in relationships, at times, is that we don't allow enough time for the person to play the Big Joker. We don't allow enough time and enough situations to unfold for us to see how this person really deals with certain emotions and issues. And, at times, that person can be a master at hiding the Crazy Card…without even knowing it.

WE'RE ALL A LITTLE CRAZY

The popular singer Seal had a hit song called "Crazy." In that song, Seal has a line that says, "No, we're never gonna survive unless we get a little crazy." Key word here is *little*. I believe we're all a *little* crazy. It helps the world stay interesting. Actually, I believe we're all crazy because of our parents, where we were born, our friends, our first loves, our schools and our experiences…our lives as a whole. We are all different, so you can never expect someone to handle things the way you do. This goes back to individuality, and when relating to one another the craziness will eventually come out. Of course, it would be a wonderful world if we all revealed the things that may be crazy about us, or what will make us go crazy. Sadly, our crazy is not always good and conducive to moving forward in life. Our past hurts and pains don't make a very good foundation for the next relationship to be successful. But, if handled right, they are the things that help us get better as we grow from them and because of them.

THE CRAZIES

Here are some things people go through, that when brought up later in the relationship can become a BIG Joker!

"But...Naked Honest?"

- **Anger**—How do you or the person you're with deal with anger? Do you have a bad, uncontrollable temper? Do you get violent? Do they shut down? These are important things to know because, as sure as there is a tomorrow, something will happen that may make you angry. And, if you realize you've had a problem in the past with your temper, it would be more than fair to let your new friend know. Though it may be hard, you owe it yourself to be honest. That's right! If you're not willing to deal with your bad temper or anger issues for yourself first, you may never feel the need to let someone you just met know about it. A lot of times, we think we're protecting the people around us and ourselves by not revealing certain issues we have. But, I believe, each time we reveal something we're trying to overcome, we lessen its power. We weaken the very thing that seems to have a stronghold on us. And who knows, this person may have overcome a bad temper and may have some tips they will share with you.

- **Depression**—Depression can be a hard topic to discuss and even bring up because, I believe, most people suffering from depression don't know that they are. Some people have felt solemn, sad and melancholy so much that they take it as normal. Many people even put on a happy-go-lucky front and a smiling face out in public, yet when they get home, they crawl back into their cave of depression. For fifteen years of my life, I lived in a house with a depressed man and didn't realize what he was going through until years later. My father was dealing with depression right in front of my eyes and I didn't know it. He seemed lazy and lethargic around the house, and like many people dealing with depression, he turned to alcohol and drugs. But to meet him you may think he was fine. Years later, it was in a conversation that he admitted to being depressed. After that conversation, our talks were more revealing than ever before. My father seemed to find a sense of relief in talking about something that had been plaguing him for years. Depression can be mild or very serious and debilitating to one's life. If you feel like you may be suffering from depression, help is available. Talk to someone you trust or search online for treatment facilities or therapists in your area.

- **Lingering Negative Relationships**—I can sum this one up by saying ANYONE WHO BRINGS MAJOR DRAMA WITH THEM WHENEVER YOU SEE OR TALK TO THEM. And let me rephrase that…drama period. Some people may bring a little drama, always in a bad mood, gossiping all the time, or always in need of help. Relationships that aren't profitable and enriching to both people involved will always put a strain on the person who's doing better. Of course, there are friends and associates you had before you met your new friend. But, as your new relationship progresses, you have to do an evaluation of whether or not your past relationships will bring problems into your new one. If you had "Baby Mama" or "Baby Daddy" drama before you met your new boo, you may want to let them know ahead of time. Or, if you had friends that were rowdy and always falling into trouble, any relationship that caused trouble in your life before, if not dealt with properly, can cause problems again. Do yourself and your new mate a favor and try to sweep away the messy folks as early as you can.

- **Criminal Activity**—No one is perfect, but not everyone has a criminal record either. This one is only bad if you hide it. We live in a society that tends to be lenient on people with criminal pasts; when it comes to certain crimes. If you are a person with a criminal past, even if it's Jaywalking, bring it to the table. If the crime is less serious, it probably will be a funny story that you and your mate will laugh about. But, if your crime was something harsher, the best you can do is be honest and hope you're not judged by your past

"But...Naked Honest?"

mistake. Either way, you want to bring it up as early in the relationship as possible and hope for the best.

- **Food and Faith**—Okay...stop laughing! These two things are very important to discuss. And, people get fanatical about them both! I've met vegans who will humiliate and disgust you with their meat horror stories if they know you're a carnivore. And I've met Christians more radical than Muslim extremists when it comes to condemning those who break one of the Ten Commandments. I believe life is about finding balance. Finding balance in every little or big aspect of our lives helps us to flow in a greater appreciation for every part of our lives. It is important to know what your new mate likes to eat and doesn't like to eat because it will affect where you go for meals, what you buy for groceries and your overall health and fitness regimen. It is important to know your new mate's faith practices because it will

The Big Joker aka The Crazy Card

determine how you worship and pray in and out of your home and sanctuary. It will also determine your overall lifestyle together, the moral do's and don'ts of your new friend and if you are cool with them.

- **STDs**—There's nothing like being in a relationship with someone, especially a sexual relationship, and finding out later in the relationship that your mate has an STD. I am speaking from experience. As crazy as this may sound, this happened to me twice. Now you may be asking, "How in the world would someone not tell the person they're about to have sex with that they have an STD?" I'm not making excuses for these people, but in their cases both women had attracted Herpes at an early age, and after their initial outbreaks they went years without any outbreaks. Sadly, because of the shame and embarrassment associated with this and any STD, many people hide it, and in their cases, it's easy to hide something when you can't see

"But...Naked Honest?"

it. Thankfully, they didn't pass it on to me, but their misconception was, like that of a lot of people, that if there is no outbreak then they couldn't pass it on. Which, if you study about Herpes and several other diseases (like HPV), you find out that this is not true. You can pass on a disease without an outbreak. If you contract a STD or STI (sexually transmitted disease or sexually transmitted infection) before or even during your relationship, it is your duty to inform your partner. That's it. Deal with the shame and guilt later. This is about the safety and well-being of others. It's also about giving your partner the right to choose! That's right! Every STD or STI isn't a death sentence, and you never know what a person is willing to deal with until you give that person the right to choose. To this day, I'm still friends them, but a part of our relationship was permanently damaged because my trust was broken. Don't endanger someone's health and well-being, and don't take away their right to choose. Get tested, be informed and inform your partner of your health status before you have sex.

- **Debt**—I've heard it said that the two leading causes of divorce in America are sexual issues and money issues. And, to me, sex is easier to discuss. I'm serious! I can walk down Hollywood Boulevard and ask people 10 sex questions and they'd laugh, joke and get involved. Yet, let me ask those same people about their bank accounts and they'd probably call me a few names and run. It's not always easy to talk about money, especially if you have debt. The larger the debt, the harder it is to discuss. But, eventually, you have to talk about your financial situation with your mate, especially if you two are getting serious, and start purchasing things together. Finances are hard to talk about because we're so deeply tied to our money. How we earn and spend our money defines us in a lot of ways. I know people who make a great deal of money and spend it as fast

"But...Naked Honest?"

as they make it, so in turn, they have to make a great deal more. And, I know people who don't make a lot of money, yet they are wise stewards over what they have and seem to be the wealthiest people I know. Complete and peaceful. Whatever your financial state let your mate know when it's time (usually before you rent an apartment or buy a house together). This will get rid of those hardcore, scary surprises like there being a padlock on your front door or a repo man towing away your car. If you and your mate are going to build together, you should set and establish how you're going to handle finances in your household, as a part of your future goals discussion. Find what works best for your union and stick to it.

All in all, you want to have enough information to make a sound decision on whether you can handle what comes next. Not that you'll be able to predict the future by someone's past or present state of mind or being, but

The Big Joker aka The Crazy Card

at least you'll be able to say and know you both started with a fair knowledge of who you were dealing with. And, if you're the one dropping a Big Joker, know that the fact that you chose to be open and honest about your issues shows that you're ready to try to make this new relationship work. Kudos!

Chapter 8

The Beef

I HAVE TO BE HONEST FOLKS. I do not like arguing. I don't like fighting. I fight with enemies not friends. And when it's over, my enemy will be defeated. Okay…sounds like I play too many video games or something, right? I just really hate bickering and arguing. I can't even take someone raising a voice at me. So, anyone I deal with in a relationship has to know that I could end our relationship over an argument. And, that could be hard for them to understand if in their past relationships they could argue with their mate and still function like a normal couple. Tell me, who's better off, the person that can't argue or the person that can argue and move on? It all comes down to what you and your mate decide works best for the two of you. What's your compromise point, rules of arguing, and when do you agree to disagree and let it go? When you're in a relationship with someone other than yourself, it is inevitable that you two will have a disagreement. Here are some things to consider prior to "The Beef" that may help you diffuse the situation.

ARE YOU LOOKING FOR A REASON

Have you ever met someone that always seems to be on the edge? They always seem to have one nerve left and everyone is standing on it. They say things like, "Oh…I thought I was gonna have to go off!" or "Don't make me go off…" or "I almost cussed them out!" Or, maybe they always seemed easily offended or defensive. What about the person who likes to instigate controversy just to get into a confrontation? Every now and then, we meet people who seem to be looking for a reason to argue and fight. It's as if they're not happy unless there's some friction sparking a fire of fury. Hopefully, you won't have to get too far into your new relationship before you realize whether you're with this type of person. The sooner you realize who you're with the sooner you can decide if you're cool with their explosive attitude or not.

TRIGGERS AND PAIN BODIES

In the process of getting to know your new friend/mate, be sure to listen for anything that may be a Trigger or Pain Body. TRIGGERS AND PAIN BODIES are things that conjure up the memory of a painful moment in that person's life. A memory that may cause them to become defensive, hurt, angry, sad, or even violent. Bad relationships, abuse, and neglect can leave painful imprints on our minds that are hard to shake and overcome. The scary thing is you don't have to be in an argument with someone to pull a Trigger or push a Pain Body button. In fact, you could think that you're doing something good for the person or encouraging them, and something you say or do brings back a dark, upsetting memory. Of course, it also helps if your friend already knows what their Triggers are. Just as the right type of communication can cause a relationship to flourish, in this case, saying something that is taken in the wrong context can start a battle. As these triggers and pain bodies are revealed, take time to talk about where they come from. This type of dialogue can lead you into a whole new level of friendship and understanding with your mate. By knowing better, you'll be mindful of doing better when talking to your mate.

FAIR FIGHT

As much as we try to avoid arguments and disagreements, it's inevitable that they will occur. So, before you get into a hardcore war of words, be sure to set your Fair

The Beef

Fighting Rules. There has to be some ground rules for when those arguments occur that will keep you and your mate from saying or doing something that you could regret later. Here are some rules you may want to consider when making your Fair Fighting Checklist:

- VOLUME—Set a voice level when you two are in a great mood. "Alright honey, we can't talk louder than this when having a disagreement." This is a big one. If you can control your voices while arguing, believe me, your argument will lose steam quickly.

- LISTEN TO HEAR—I know it's hard to listen intently when you're waiting and trying to get your point across, but I've learned that most times we're not really hearing what our mate is trying to say. We're really missing their point in the moment of intensity and anger. A great technique I've learned is to ask one simple question: "What did you hear me say?" Usually, they heard something totally different from what you meant. "I heard you say I was STUPID!" she says. "No, baby, I said this is stupid; us arguing over that movie." Believe it or not, that simple question, if you let it sink in, will also show you how your mate perceives what you say before they even hear what you actually say. AND, LET ME REITERATE, if you can do any of these techniques prior to your argument, it will do wonders for you and your mate. Try practicing while having dinner or coffee. See how many times during the course of a day that something you said is heard another way from what you meant. It may shock you.

- WE'RE NOT GOING TO BED ANGRY—Whether you two are at the place where you're sharing a bed or you fall asleep together holding your cellphones to your ears while at your own separate homes, don't go to bed angry! Make that a rule and you'll find a way to solve problems before nightfall. This classic rule is one worth practicing immediately, even if you're not in a relationship with anyone. A guilt–free, pleasant night's sleep usually leads to a happy fresh-start morning. Every day will have its own worries and stressful events for you to conquer. Why add to the next day's tasks and issues with a lingering argument?

Incorporating these three techniques into your Fair Fighting Rules will make a huge difference in not only how you argue but how you approach a disagreement with your mate.

IS IT WORTH IT

An intelligent person once said, "Choose your battles wisely." I echo that statement. When it comes to getting into a "heated discussion" with your mate, try to decide early on if it's worth it or not. Is this discussion really worth upsetting your mate and yourself? From my own personal experience, everything is magnified when you're in a relationship with someone, especially when you're around that person every day.

"But...Naked Honest?"

"So you're just gonna leave the toothpaste cap on the counter, huh?" she says.

"Hun, your pantyhose are waving at me, can you warn me next time you let them air dry in the bathroom, huh?" he says.

"This trash won't take itself out..."

"I didn't make these dishes..."

"Where's dinner?"

These simple things can come up every day. These small things can be the fuse to the stick of dynamite that will damage, if not destroy, a shaky foundation. A small argument with a serious topic, or fault thrown in, can create a battle. That battle can turn into a war. To prevent the small stuff from escalating into something big, try to put issues into proper perspective before you bring it up to your mate. For example, if the cap is off the toothpaste, and that is a pet peeve of yours, you have to think consequently. If you go off about the toothpaste cap,

The Beef

and then your mate goes off in defense, you have a fight. The fight pisses you both off. He has an ulcer, she has a migraine, one of you brings up a past issue to reinforce your point, and then one of you calls the other a name and then you talk about your mate's mother and then... PUT THE CAP ON YOURSELF! Your relationship is, and will always be, about compromise! One of you will always be lacking something and that is where the other should step in and say, "I got that." Have each other's back and rejoice in that. If you take on a mentality of service for one another and learn to celebrate one another, you'll find that you'll actually LOVE doing for one another. Being kind and GOING OUT OF YOUR WAY for your mate will be a pleasure, and hopefully, they will do the same. GOING OUT OF YOUR WAY means doing something you didn't plan on doing, you don't normally do or maybe didn't want to do for your mate to bring harmony in your relationship because you care about them and you care about yourself.

"But...Naked Honest?"

We must realize that to truly love and care for someone beyond ourselves, we must truly and confidently love and care about ourselves. Then serving your mate will be a pleasure, ladies and gentlemen, not a chore. And, hopefully, it's a mutual pleasure.

Chapter 9

The Decision

I REALIZE THAT MANY OF YOU may have already made your decision on whether or not you're going to continue your relationship or if you want to pursue one before Chapter 9. If you haven't, then this chapter of the book may help you make one of three decisions that you'll have to make throughout your whole relationship.

- **STOP**—Stop your new relationship when:

    The person doesn't respect you—If your new friend shows you from the beginning that they don't respect your time, space, presence, property, energy or opinion, then why would you stay?

The person is an abuser—They abuse drugs, alcohol, themselves, children, the dog, the cat, you, money... leave them alone! Physically, sexually, mentally, spiritually, emotionally, financially abusive people don't need you... they need therapy.

The person lies—If you two haven't been together a month, and they've told you three lies...STOP! Always hold yourself in high regard. If these are a person's habits, let them go!

- **SLOW DOWN**—These days, we need everything right now. I remember when if someone called your home and you were not there, that was it. Hopefully, you had an answering machine so they could leave a message. If not, they would have to wait until you got in. Nowadays, someone will text you and before you can text them back they will call to ask, "Did you get my text?" We're a very IMMEDIATELY society that hates to wait. And in relationship building, the most important thing is not moving too fast. Be patient. We make PATIENCE a dirty eight-letter, two-syllable word. If we take our time and get to know our new friends before jumping into a serious relationship, we would avoid so much heartache and pain. Slow down when "you're just not sure yet." There's no need to rush things. If it's meant to be, it will be.

- **GO, GO, GO!**—At my forums and shows, I always say to people, "You betta be giddy and happy-go-lucky in the beginning of your relationship!" I believe that wholeheartedly. There will be enough obstacles down the road of your relationship, why start with obstacles, and warning and caution signs piled up in front of you? Don't go down that road. Why do we settle for less than happiness at the very beginning of

"But...Naked Honest?"

a relationship when you have no obligation to commit to this person? If you are happy, and this person has you on Cloud Nine and they respect and honor you, and have qualities that are essential to your life and happiness, GO FOR IT! Keep the train moving and see where it takes you.

What I want you to take away from this book is knowing there is a way to talk about everything you have been through and go through in life. Don't be afraid to ask and answer questions about life. There are no wrong questions if you truly want to know the answers. But, remember, we're not initiating interrogations. We're practicing "Conversational *Peace*" and having fun while learning about others and ourselves. I hope this book made you laugh and think. Thank you for taking time to read it. Thank you for considering my thoughts important enough to occupy some space in your beautiful mind. Remember, whether you're single, in a new relationship,

The Decision

or have been married thirty years, you should never stop dating. You should never stop getting to know yourself and the wonderful person you've chosen to be with. Find new things to do on your dates. Keep it fresh and fun! Until next time, God Bless, One Love.

Chapter 10
Bonus Blogs

*Sex & Love: RAW UNCUT
with Troy Rawlings*

FOR SEVERAL YEARS, I'VE BEEN WRITING blogs based on my thoughts on different aspects of relationships. My online friends always send me questions and topics about sex, love, relationships and everything in between. So I try to educate and entertain from my comedic knowledge. If I can make you laugh and make you say, "Hmmmm, good point," then my mission is accomplished! Here are some of my thoughts on some adult relationship topics. Enjoy!

I WANNA TEXT YOU UP!

"Is texting the same as calling?"

Simply put…NO! In the search for the answer to that age-old question, "How do I know if he likes me?" I replied, "Does he like to be around you? Does he call you at least six to seven times a week, asking you for a date just because he can't wait to be near you? If so he probably likes you!" Most men are pretty simple. We're easy to figure out for the most part. We're hungry—feed us. We're horny—fuck us. We're happy—we want to keep doing the exact thing that makes us happy. And if that thing is being with you, you'll know.

In our Microwave-gimme-now-society, texting has made communication convenient. In some cases, that's cool. If you're at work and need to get a message to someone and can't call them, or if you just want to send a quick message, even fun flirting, then texting is perfect.

But when you find yourself having full conversations with your fingers instead of taking the same time to pick up a phone and call someone, then you have lost a very important component of the human experience, which is expression of emotion.

Our emotions and expressions convey so much in our daily conversations, as well as in the things we don't say while on the phone. Those "awkward silences" when just hearing the person's breathing can soothe you. In 2013, it seems that personal touch can be an evasive and rare treat…it used to be normal.

The great thing about texting is that you can say all the freaky or mean stuff you've always wanted to say, and as long as you follow it with "LOL," it's ALL GOOD! Actually, writing a letter, with pen and paper, is still very romantic. There's something about the strokes of the pen that carry weight and feeling more than a digital font. Ladies and gents, take time out and buy a blank greeting card, and write what you feel. Don't even try to make it

"But...Naked Honest?"

sound polished. Shit, it can say... *The way you lick me is unreal! See you later! Love, Condalisa.* I guarantee it will garner a passionate response or two.

Another thing you could try is leaving more texts that are open-ended. Let your partner know you'll finish them later. For example, "When we see each other later, I have a surprise for you." Build up some suspense with your texts, but always make the in-person encounter more substantial than what you wrote. You could actually play a game where you sit across from each other, write down your wildest questions and watch the person's facial expressions as they answer in writing and then switch papers. This game can go on until the passionate messages get so hot that someone says, "Check please!"

I guess as long as your homie, lover, friend knows they are the apple of your eye, and your cell phone, it's cool. LOL!

THE 20-YEAR VIRGIN

"Man, I've been married 20 years; I wouldn't even know how to approach a woman to ask her out on a date…"

It's not always like falling down off a bicycle. More like being thrown off a horse, a Clydesdale even. Jumping into the new millennium-dating scene after a divorce is hard enough. But when you've been with the same person for almost half your life or more, it can seem hard trying to meet someone new. Men and women struggle every day with trying not to compare their new partner to their old partner. After being married to someone for 20 years, unless you were having affairs throughout your 20 years, this person was all you knew. If times were good, you share them with that person. In the bad times, you either cried together or comforted each other. And, in the ugly times, that was the person you wanted to choke! Well… not really, hopefully it didn't get there. But, the question is *"How do I date now?"*

"But...Naked Honest?"

A better question is, *"Do you want to date now?"* Though loneliness and the need for companionship may be kicking your ass, depending on how tumultuous your break up was, you might need to take some time by yourself to find yourself. Time to find out who you really are and what you really want. Time to heal. Time to love yourself to the point that having a mate enhances you; not make you become someone else, or even worse, become what someone else wants you to be. Time is a remedy, a cure, and a healing balm like no other. I've heard it said, "Time heals all wounds." I don't know about ALL, but time sure helps.

There is no right way to approach someone you're interested in. It's always good to: *#1. Make Eye Contact (don't stare) and right before it becomes a creepy stare, #2. Say hello!* Hopefully you're not antisocial and can carry a conversation with this person. I take it the hard part is possibly meeting that person's "Representative" first. Getting past all the smoke and mirrors to try and get to the genuine article. And even if this person is transparent with you and says, "Ask me anything you wish…I'll answer honestly!" you still have to spend time with a person to know how they act from day to day and in different scenarios. The process of learning someone new…UGGGGGGHHHH!

The armed forces would never allow someone back into public life after 20 years of war without deprogramming them. So, how successful do you really think you'll be, trying to date after 20 years of marriage without taking time to deprogram from your ex? And that simply means time to heal. How long that takes, no one knows. Everyone is different. But give yourself time and space. Space from the playing field. Yep. The relationship "Game" can be brutal and wonderful at the same time. But a wounded player…always gets sidelined. One of the best things you can do is to examine every part of you—weaknesses, strengths—and that in you which is SUPERHUMAN. I know it sounds corny, but what makes

"But...Naked Honest?"

you stand out from the pack? What makes you a prize? You have to regain your confidence, and know your self worth, so you won't bring anyone else down, rather you would always encourage greatness.

If you do these things, when you're ready to get back out there…you'll know.

Bonus Blogs

BUT PRINCE STILL DOES IT!
(Feminine Masculinity)

Ever heard a woman talk about how off the hook a guy is? "He's fine, he's funny, he can dress his ass off... he...he..." and then say "BUT I THINK HE'S GAY?!" Then with a little investigation, you find out the guy has a wife, girlfriend, kids, a pit-bull... Was he too feminine acting for people to think he was straight?

Over the years, I've noticed that men, me included, are more well groomed, compassionate, emotional, caring, sometimes moody...can cook, WTF? That's not too crazy. But what happens when a guy takes it to the next level; makeup, not getting his haircut but getting it permed, cut and colored? When he wears blouses, and all his pants are tight, he always wants you to toss his salad?! Well, maybe not the salad tossing...but, do you feel like some men are just too feminine?

"But...Naked Honest?"

Rock music fans and groupies have always loved the Rock-Star bad boys who wore makeup, tight, painted-on pants, blouses and silk scarves with high heel boots. While, of course, there may have been some Rock Stars who were bisexual and even gay, their outer persona didn't deter people from believing they were chick magnets. Prince built a whole image of *Controversy...Am I straight or gay...* and as much as comedians and others would joke about him, women still want his loins to this day! What it all boils down to is who you really are. Are you being your genuine self?

Prince is Prince twenty-four-seven. As far as we know, he's always been a little *Sexy Motherfucker*! Some guys have been raised by women, have sisters, and some are just clean freaks. Our personality is what makes us different, unique, interesting and attractive. Some women are definitely attracted to men who seem more "in touch with their feminine side." This may be because she feels like she can communicate with him better or he's more compassionate. Nowadays, some ladies like to take charge. Work, relationship, sex…girls run the world! So, the feminine-masculine dude may be just right for her.

The overall fear comes in not knowing. We tend to fear what we don't understand or can't categorize in a group, sect or race. If a woman doesn't know whether the guy she's with is heterosexual, homosexual, or bisexual, she could get a bit fearful. History has taught us not to assume anything until we know for sure. Just because a man is into Oprah, bakes cookies, and wears assless-chaps does not mean he's not all-true man! So, just ask. While you're eating that gourmet dinner he just made you and before you take that hot-bubble bath….right as he's wiping off his eyeliner, ask, "Baby, have you ever been with a man, or do you desire to?" Hopefully, he'll be honest. And for all those women who like those hardcore, macho James Dean or Rock Hudson type men…

CHEATING WITH YOUR SPOUSE

You see her laughing with someone by the bar. The nightclub is packed, but this sister is glowing in your eyes. Her body is calling your name, and you have yet to introduce yourself. As your eyes meet with hers, you realize she is attracted to you as well. You grab your drink and start walking toward her. She gently smiles, licks her lips and looks down with a devilish grin. As you come within arms reach, she looks up and says, "Hello." You return the greeting and the conversation ensues. The conversation is fun and flirtatious, so much so that your immediate infatuation causes momentary amnesia. You find yourself absent-minded. Almost forgetting to tell this lovely, sexy woman one important thing…you are married. Deciding to take a chance and put it on the table, you tell the young lady, "By the way, I am married." She looks at you and smiles, and then says, "So I guess that makes it easy… we know what we're here for." And you both continue talking, until you leave together.

Bonus Blogs

Now whether you want to believe it or not, this scenario happens every day or night somewhere in the world to a man or woman. But what if you could "flip the script," or, better yet, write the script in your favor? What if that woman or man was your wife or husband… but you two were the only ones who knew? That's right people; I'm talking about the ultimate role-play. Before a mistress or mister jacks up your marriage, why not become your mate's secret rendezvous?

You know I've always stressed open and honest communication with your mate. And while some were shocked by Monique (actress/comedian) admitting that if she or her husband had sex with someone outside of their marriage it wouldn't be a "deal breaker"; it wouldn't end their marriage, I was happy to know they were open enough to have that conversation with one another before it happened. What would the divorce rate be if more people talked about the hard situations before they happened? And better yet, explicitly told their loved ones what they

"But...Naked Honest?"

could handle and couldn't handle. But to Monique and her husband's credit, they were best friends first. And if you think about it, you're quicker to leave a mate than a best friend. Best friends are usually for life, and you can tell them anything.

Just think about it. Shouldn't the "love of your life" also be your freak on the side? If today's daily news of infidelity doesn't tell us anything else, it should drive us to be honest about our emotional and sexual needs. Everybody doesn't need a sex addict clinic...just maybe some sexual healing from their hubby or wifey, the way they want it.

I dare you to be radical about keeping your boo. Start by having that deep, intense, truthful conversation about what you do and don't like. Including what kind of man or woman turns you on. WARNING – please make sure your mate is not the crazy jealous type who may bust you upside your head after you describe his uncle! After you get open, start trying different things that you both like or just do something that your mate fantasizes about. If you want something exciting, better and different in your current relationship, you have to do something exciting better and different. Like, for example, randomly seeing each other at a breakfast spot or jogging. Act like total strangers and have a conversation. See how far it goes. Who knows, you might get lucky on the first date.

Here are a few ideas and exercises you can try to keep the excitement growing with your mate:

1. ***Share the Funny Stuff***—Remember when we were young and everyone had crazy ideas and stories about what sex was, but no one was having sex? If you and your mate get together and start talking about some of the funny, scary, and just plain stupid sex stories and myths you believed as a youngin', it will open up a whole new level of understanding and enjoyment between you and your mate.

2. *TALK TO ME, SAY THAT!*—Now I realize some of you have kids, work long hours as a professional, and are respected members of your community. Whatever! You should be able to yell out a four-letter, golden word during hot, butt-naked sex. But, just make sure your partner approves of the word. Sit down with your mate and do a list of Do Say & Don't Say words. Then once you have approval, let it rip! The next time you're hot, and ready, you'll be able to say, just what your lover would love to hear.

3. *BABY, YOU SMELL GOOD*—When was the last time you went perfume or cologne shopping? Candles, soaps, oils, incense, find out what scents turn your partner on. What scents make them relax, and what scents soothe them. Also, talk about what scents they remember from when they were younger. Try to find oils and lotions that carry the fragrance

your mate can't resist. And, rub it where you want them to go, or close to it.

Lastly, knowledge is power. Instead of picking up your favorite magazine this weekend, pick up a book on sex, love and sensuality for you and your mate. Start enhancing your relationship daily, if you want to keep it.

EYES WIDE SHUT

Since I'm always asking some kind of intimate question about sex or love, which is usually pulled from the back of my mind, or my imagination, it's no wonder this next topic boggles my mind …just a little. It's the "Why do you close your eyes during sex?" question! I'm not sure if I'm the only one bothered by this, but I know some of you are saying, "Stop being so petty, Troy… at least SEX is happening!" Umm, really? If you're just happy to be having sex, then stop reading this blog NOW. But if you're in search of sexual bliss in every two-minute quickie and one-hundred-eighty-minute Tantric session, then you feel me when I say that it all matters in our connection with one another.

"During our passionate, wet, sensual, deep love making, as I was above my lover, I noticed that her eyes were slammed shut as she moaned, as the sweat dripped from my head down to her beautiful nose…she jumped."

Bonus Blogs

LMAO… because it startled her! Why? Because she was deep in thought somewhere else! Hey, that's my opinion on the matter. We all know women are deeply emotional, wonderful, complex, and picturesque creatures. That being said, if women are highly sensual, romanticized, and sensitive to every touch…and she dreams about you… why close your eyes when you're with the man of your dreams? Don't get me wrong, I'm not saying that there aren't times when the loving is so good that you close your eyes in ecstasy, but not for the whole time!

We men usually keep our eyes open during sexual enjoyment. We want to see the ripples in your ass as we do it doggy-style, the looks of pain/pleasure on your face as we're thrusting inside you like Jason from *Friday the 13th*, to see your hair (real, unreal, short, long) as we pull it or it sticks to the sweat on your face like glue. Bottom line, all of the hot sights of sex! Men only close their eyes to think about things that will prolong their premature ejaculations. That's pretty much it. Ladies and gentlemen,

"But...Naked Honest?"

if a man closes his eyes during sex it's a compliment. If a woman closes her eyes, I think she's wondering... wondering whom she could actually be with. "Yes, yes... take it, Rock! Go deeper, Will...Work it, Emmanuel Lewis..." whatever.

So, if you want to increase the passion in your lovemaking, try looking at your lover. No matter how ugly a face they make, embrace it. Because if you close your eyes while we're having sex, I'm going to make goofy faces at you...I'm serious, sticking out my tongue, holding my nose up...the whole nine!

Until The Next Time,
Much Love
Troy
Feel free to email me your questions:
troyrawlings@gmail.com

THANK YOUS

I won't be able to thank everyone, so I won't even try. Plus, this is the first of many books so if you have been important to my life I'll mention you in some way. Let me first thank my best friend Rodney "Yonder" Harrison. Brother, we talk all the time so you know I love you. But, it was your guidance that helped bring my vision of being an author to reality. Thank you 1,000 times.

Latia N Lynch and Dee Blackmon, thank you for allowing me to be a part of your literary journey and also encouraging me to take my own.

Thank you Jessica Tilles for the perfect final touches.

Thank you Ande, and Jessica, for your honesty, expertise and most of all your light!

"But...Naked Honest?"

Thank you to all my friends and family from Baltimore to Burbank. You know who you are and what you've done.

To my great motivator, and business partner, Ertha Harris—you are my Harriet Tubman—your words move nations.

Thank you to my 12th grade English and Theatre Arts teacher, Ms. Gill, for exposing my gifts to me and then challenging me to enter the Maryland State Writing Contest. Good job!

Christal Friedman, the greatest assistant in the world... even when you can't find her, she's working lol.

Uncle Carl Bean—thank you for powerful love-filled words of wisdom.

Thank you to my brother, Mustafa Del Ali, for an example of no limits, hard work and dedication. #DriveOnandDoGood #WorkHardPlayHard.

Thank you Rahimah for my greatest gift next to being born and salvation—Zoe Troi Rawlings. We did awesome.

Thank Yous

And to my mother, Betty Jefferson—thank you for being alive. Thank you, Mom, for pulling me aside at a young age (middle school) and having the deepest, most poignant talks I would ever engage in, in my life. You changed my life, so now I hope to change the world for the better.

Love you all. And, to those I didn't mention here, like Keno, Keira, and Michelle, Ron and Bob...keep reading my books. I'll thank you more later :-)

www.ingramcontent.com/pod-product-compliance
Lightning Source LLC
Chambersburg PA
CBHW051453290426
44109CB00016B/1736